FLOWERING REEDS

DEDICATED
TO
MY MOTHER

ROY CAMPBELL

FLOWERING REEDS

poems

1933

BORISWOOD LIMITED

Republished 1971
Scholarly Press, Inc., 22929 Industrial Drive East
St. Clair Shores, Michigan 48080

Printed at The Alcuin Press
Campden: Gloucestershire

First published in 1933
by
Boriswood Limited
15a Harrington Road
London, S.W.7

Library of Congress Catalog Card Number: 78-131659
ISBN 0-403-00546-9

BY THE SAME AUTHOR
THE FLAMING TERRAPIN
THE WAYZGOOSE
ADAMASTOR
THE GEORGIAD
POMEGRANATES

FLOWERING REEDS

CONTENTS

The Flowering Reed   13

Canaan   14

Song   17

The Shell   18

Autumn Plane   19

The Flame   20

The Road to Arles   21

The Flower   22

The Blue Wave   23

Wings   24

Swans   25

Vespers on the Nile   26

On the top of the Caderau   28

Choosing a Mast   29

The Secret Muse   32

The Rejoneador   33

La Clemence   34

Reflection   35

The Louse Catchers (after Rimbaud)   36

The Olive Tree (I)   38

The Olive Tree (II)   39

A Sleeping Woman   40

The Albatross (after Baudelaire)   41

The Gum Trees   42

Overtime   46

THE FLOWERING REED

WHEN the red brands of day consume
  And in the darkening Rhone illume
The still reflections of the reed,
I saw its passing leagues of gloom,
Torrential in their strength and speed,
Resisted by a rosy plume
That burned far down among the weed;
As in the dark of Tullia's tomb
The frail wick-tethered phantom set
To watch, remember and regret,
Thawing faint tears to feed its fume
Of incense, spent in one long sigh
The centuries that thundered by
To battle, scooping huge moraines
Across the wreck of fifty reigns;
It held a candle to the eye
To show how much must pass and die
To set such scatheless phantoms free,
Or feather with one reed of rhyme
The boulder-rolling Rhone of time,
That rafts our ruin to the sea.

CANAAN

BENEATH us stream the golden hours
The slower for our hearts, where now,
Two ripe grenades on the same bough,
Their globes of bronze together swung,
Have stayed the stream they overhung
With fallen heaps of flowers.

For never was she half so fair
Whose colours bleed the red rose white
And milk the lilies of their light:
In her snowed breasts where sorrow dies,
All the white rills of Canaan rise,
And cedars in her hair.

Half-way across a flowery land
Through which our still reluctant feet
Must pass, for every halt too fleet,
We pause upon the topmost hill
Whence streams of wine and honey spill
To some rapacious strand.

There, sisters of the milky way,
The rills of Canaan sing and shine:
Diluvial in the waves of wine

14

Whose gulls are rosy-footed doves
The glorious bodies of my loves
Like dolphins heave the spray—

Red Rhones towards the sounding shore
Through castled gorges roaring down
By many a tiered and towery town,
High swollen with a spate of hours,
And strewn with all the dying flowers
That we shall love no more—

Torrential in the nightingale,
My spirit hymns them as they go
For wider yet their streams must flow
With flowery trophies heaped more high
Before they drain their sources dry
And those clear fountains fail.

I cannot think (so blue the day)
That those fair castalies of dreams
Or the cool naiads of their streams,
Or I, the willow in whose shade
Their wandering music was delayed,
Should pass like ghosts away.

The azure triumphs on the height:

Life is sustained with golden arms:
The fire-red cock with loud alarms
Arising, drums his golden wings
And in the victory he sings,
The Sun insults the night.

O flying hair and limbs of fire
Through whose frail forms, that fade and pass,
Tornadoing as flame through grass,
Eternal beauty flares alone
To build herself a blazing throne
Out of the world's desire—

The summer leaves are whirled away:
The fallen chestnut in the grass
Is trampled by the feet that pass
And like the young Madonna's heart
With rosy portals gashed apart
Bleeds for the things I say.

SONG

YOU ask what far-off singing
   Has mingled with our rest.
It is my love that, winging
The deep wave of your breast,
With white sail homeward turning,
Sings at the golden oar
Of a white city burning
On the battle-tented shore.

THE SHELL

THE azure films upon her eyes
  Are folded like the wings of terns;
But still the wavering tide returns,
And in her hair an ocean sighs:
Still in her flesh the Anger glows
And in her breathing seems to hiss
The phantom of the fiercest kiss
With which we slew its crimson rose—
As in a flushed barbaric shell
Whose lips of coral, sharked with pearls,
Of the remembered surges tell,
A ghostly siren swells the roar
And sings of some deserted shore
Within whose caves the ocean swirls.

AUTUMN PLANE

PEELED white and washed with fallen rain,
  A dancer weighed with jingling pearls,
The girl-white body of a plane
In whose red hair the Autumn swirls
Stands out soliciting the cruel
Flame of the wintry sun, and dies
If only to the watcher's eyes
In red-gold anguish glowing; fuel
To that cold fire as she assumes
(Brunhilde) her refulgent plumes
In leaves that kindle as they die.
Of all that triumphs and returns
The furious aurora burns
Against the winter-boding sky.

THE FLAME

IN the blue darkness of your hair,
Smouldering on from birth to death,
My love is like the burnish there
That I can kindle with a breath.
Or like the flame in this black wine
Upon whose raven wings we rise
Lighter in spirit than the sighs
With which the purple roses twine:
Like a great star with steady beam
It runs against a darkened stream,
And from its onrush of despairs
Draws all the splendours of my blood,
As I have seen the Rhone in flood
Drawn starward by the golden hairs.

THE ROAD TO ARLES

FROM the cold huntress shorn of any veil
　Bare trees, the target of her silver spite,
Down the long avenue in staggy flight
Are hunted by the hungers of the gale:
Along the cold grey torrent of the sky
Where branch the fatal trophies of his brows,
Actæon, antlered in the wintry boughs,
Rears to the stars his mastiff-throttled cry.
Pride has avenging arrows for the eyes
That strip her beauty silver of disguise,
And she has dogs before whose pace to flee—
In front a waste, behind a bended bow,
And a long race across the stony Crau
Torn in each gust, and slain in every tree.

THE FLOWER

LET no light word your silence mar:
This one red flame be all you say,
Between the old and new desire
A solitary point of fire,
The hesitation of a star
Between the twilight and the day.

So rich the pollen of your breath
It is sufficient to be dumb,
Foreknowing, as the moment slips,
That in the parting of our lips
The hour has slain a rose whose death
Will colour all our days to come.

THE BLUE WAVE

THE blue wave resembles
   The moment we hold
By its tresses of gold,
For it flushes and trembles,
And is drawn by the fiery
Low sun from the sea
Where his sister and he,
Sailing home to their eyrie
Like eagles to nest,
Bear it on like the hour
That we hold in our power,
When the day like a dragon
Has sunken its crest,
And the star in our flagon
Is that in the West.

WINGS

WHEN gathering vapours climb in storm
The steep sierras of delight,
Wings of your hair I love to form
And on its perfume soar from sight.
For in those great black plumes unfurled
The darkest condor of my thought
May stretch his aching sinews taut
And fling his shadow on the world.
When sick of self my moods rebel,
The demon from his secret hell,
The eagle from his cage of brass,
They have been lent such scented wings
Over the wreck of earthly things
In silence with the sun to pass.

SWANS

THE dark trees slept, none to the azure true,
  Save where alone, the glory of the glade,
The cone of one tall cypress cut the blue
And azure on the marble dreamed its shade:
As long as I could feel it next to mine
Her body was illumined by my ghost,
As through the silver of the lighted host
Might flush the ruby reflex of the wine.
The night ran like a river deep and blue:
The reeds of thought, with humming silver wands,
Brushed by our silence like a fleet of swans,
Sang to the passing wave their faint adieu.
Stars in that current quenched their dying flame
Like folding flowers: till down the silent streams,
Swan-drawn among the lilies, slumber came,
Veiling with rosy hand the lamp of dreams.

VESPERS ON THE NILE

WHEN to their roost the sacred ibis file,
　　Mosquito-thin against the fading West,
And palm-trees fishing in the crimson Nile
Dangle their windless effigies of rest,

Scarce to the moon's hushed conquest of the blue
Have waked the wingless warblers of the bogs,
Or to the lunar sabbath staunchly true
The jackals sung their first selenologues,

When through the waste, far-flung as from a steeple
First in low rumours, then in sounding choir,
The lamentation of an ancient people
Sounds from the waters and the sands of fire;

And centuries have heard that plaint persist,
Since Pharaoh's foreman stood with lifted quirt,
Or swung the bloody sjambok in his fist
To cut the sluggard through his hairy shirt.

This was the strain, the Amphionic lyre,
By which were carted Thebes' colossal stones,
Which though it lifted pyramid and spire
Yet rang their ruin in prophetic tones.

Still theirs the agony, still theirs the bondage,
Still theirs the toil, their recompense forlorn
To crop the thistles, bite the withered frondage
And rasp the bitter stubble of the corn.

Still as if Pharaoh's sjambok cut their rumps,
Sick for some Zion of the vast inane,
The effort of a thousand rusty pumps
Wheezes untiring through their shrill refrain.

Where royal suns descending left no stains,
Where forms of power and beauty change and pass,
One epic to eternity remains—
The heehawhallelujahs of the Ass.

ON THE TOP OF THE CADERAU

THE splintering hail of the night was continued
By the shimmering beams of a morning that
sinewed
The lowlands with silver, and trawled to the plains,
Rill-threaded, the sweep of its glittering seines:
As we rode to the summit (high over a cliff
It would dizzy the kestrel to plummet) the wind
was a stiff
Bee-line to the sun, that it flew like a thundering
kite,
Tunny-finned, and humming with gems, in the
ocean of light.
And red on the blue-black blinding azure, your coat
Like a banner of fire in the storming of heaven afloat,
A flaunted bright challenge was swung for the sun-
beam to gore
By the jewelled Aquilon, a glittering toreador;
And under the blue-black buffeted rook of your hair
Your face was a silvery cry in the solitude there,
As you reared your white horse on the summit re-
minding me this—
That the steepest nevadas of rapture rise over the
deepest abyss.

CHOOSING A MAST

THIS mast, new-shaved, through whom I rive
    the ropes,
Says she was once an oread of the slopes,
Graceful and tall upon the rocky highlands,
A slender tree as vertical as noon,
And her low voice was lovely as the silence
Through which a fountain whistles to the moon,
Who now of the white spray must take the veil
And, for her songs, the thunder of the sail.

I chose her for her fragrance, when the spring
With sweetest resins swelled her fourteenth ring
And with live amber welded her young thews:
I chose her for the glory of the Muse,
Smoother of forms, that her hard-knotted grain,
Grazed by the chisel, shaven by the plane,
Might from the steel as cool a burnish take
As from the bladed moon a windless lake.

I chose her for her eargerness of flight
Where she stood tiptoe on the rocky height
Lifted by her own perfume to the sun,
While through her rustling plumes with eager sound
Her eagle spirit, with the gale at one,

Spreading wide pinions, would have spurned the
    ground
And her own sleeping shadow, had they not
With thymy fragrance charmed her to the spot.

Lover of song, I chose this mountain pine
Not only for the straightness of her spine
But for her songs: for there she loved to sing
Through a long noon's repose of wave and wing,
The fluvial swirling of her scented hair
Sole rill of song in all that windless air,
And her slim form the naiad of the stream
Afloat upon the languor of its theme;

And for the soldier's fare on which she fed:
Her wine the azure, and the snow her bread;
And for her stormy watches on the height,
For only out of solitude or strife
Are born the sons of valour and delight;
That with the wind stopped not its singing breath
But carolled on, the louder for its death.

Under a pine, when summer days were deep,
We loved the most to lie in love or sleep:
And when in long hexameters the west
Rolled his grey surge, the forest for his lyre,

It was the pines that sang us to our rest,
Loud in the wind and fragrant in the fire,
With legioned voices swelling all night long,
From Pelion to Provence, their storm of song.

It was the pines that fanned us in the heat,
The pines, that cheered us in the time of sleet,
For which sweet gifts I set one dryad free;
No longer to the wind a rooted foe,
This nymph shall wander where she longs to be
And with the blue north wind arise and go,
A silver huntress with the moon to run
And fly through rainbows with the rising sun;

And when to pasture in the glittering shoals
The guardian mistral drives his thundering foals,
And when like Tartar horsemen racing free
We ride the snorting fillies of the sea,
My pine shall be the archer of the gale
While on the bending willow curves the sail
From whose great bow the long keel shooting home
Shall fly, the feathered arrow of the foam.

THE SECRET MUSE

BETWEEN the midnight and the morn,
To share my watches late and lonely,
There dawns a presence such as only
Of perfect silence can be born.
On the blank parchment falls the glow
Of more than daybreak: and one regal
Thought like the shadow of an eagle
Grazes the smoothness of its snow.
Though veiled to me that face of faces
And still that form eludes my art,
Yet all the gifts my faith has brought
Along the secret stair of thought
Have come to me on those hushed paces
Whose footfall is my beating heart.

THE REJONEADOR

WHILE in your lightly-veering course
   A seraph seems to take his flight,
The swervings of your snowy horse,
Volted with valour and delight,
In thundering orbit wheel the Ring
Which Apis pivots with his pain
And of whose realm, with royal stain,
His agony anoints you king.
His horns the moon, his hue the night,
The dying embers of his sight
Across their bloody film may view
The star of morning rise in fire,
Projectile of the same desire
Whose pride is animate in you.

LA CLEMENCE

WHEN with white wings and rhyme of rapid oars
The sisters of your speed, as fleet as you,
With silver scythes, the reapers of the blue,
Turn from their harvest to the sunset shores;

When the pine-heaving mistral rolls afar
The sounding gust that your stiff pinion loves,
And rose-lit sails, a thousand homing doves
With foamy ribbons draw the wave-born Star;

May you be first her rising torch to greet
And first within the distant port to ride,
Your triangle of silver for her guide,
Your pearling prow a sandal to her feet.

REFLECTION

MY thought has learned the lucid art
By which the willows lave their limbs,
Whose form upon the water swims
Though in the air they rise apart.
For when in beauty's light I lie,
By purest reason unreproved
Psyche usurps the outward eye
To trace her inward sculpture grooved
In one melodious line, whose flow
With eddying circle now invests
The rippled silver of her breasts,
Now shaves a flank of rose-lit snow,
Or rounds a cheek where sunset dies
In the black starlight of her eyes.

THE LOUSE CATCHERS
(after Rimbaud)

WHEN the child's brow, with torment flushing red,
Implores white dreams to shed their hazy veils,
Two sisters, tall and fair, approach his bed
Whose fingers glint with silver-pointed nails.

They seat him by a window, where the blue
Air bathes a sheaf of flowers: with rhythms calm,
Into his heavy hair where falls the dew,
Prowl their long fingers terrible in charm.

He hears their breathing whistle in long sighs
Flowering with ghostly pollen; and the hiss
Of spittle on the lips withdrawn, where dies
From time to time the fancy of a kiss.

Brushing cool cheeks their feathered lashes flick
The perfumed silences: through drifting veils
He hears their soft electric fingers click
The death of tiny lice with regal nails.

Drowsed in the deep wines of forgetfulness,
Delirious harmonies his spirit hears
And to the rhythm of their slow caress
Wavers and pauses on the verge of tears.

THE OLIVE TREE (I)

IN a bare country shorn of leaf,
By no remote sierra screened,
Where pauses in the wind are brief
As the remorses of a fiend,
The stark Laocoon this tree
Forms of its knotted arm and thigh
In snaky tussle with a sky
Whose hatred is eternity,
Through his white fronds that whirl and seethe
And in the groaning root he screws,
Makes heard the cry of all who breathe,
Repulsing and accusing still
The Enemy who shaped his thews
And is inherent to his will.

THE OLIVE TREE (II)

CURBED athlete hopeless of the palm,
If in the rising moon he hold,
Discobolos, a quoit of gold
Caught in his gusty sweep of arm,
Or if he loom against the dawn,
The circle where he takes his run
To hurl the discus of the sun
Is by his own dark shadow drawn:
The strict arena of his game
Whose endless effort is denied
More room for victory or pride
Than what he covers with his shame.

À SLEEPING WOMAN

REDDENING through the gems of frost
That twinkle on the milk-white thorn,
Softly hesitates the morn
In whom as yet no star is lost.
From skies the colour of her skin,
So touched with golden down, so fair,
Where glittering cypress seems to spin
The black refulgence of her hair,
Clear as a glass the day replies
To every feature save her eyes
But shows their lashes long and fine
Across her cheek by slumber drawn,
As the black needles of the pine
Are feathered on the flush of dawn.

THE ALBATROSS (after Baudelaire)

SOMETIMES, for sport, the men of loafing crews
Snare the great albatrosses of the spray
That, indolent companions of their cruise,
Pursue the gliding vessels on their way.

Scarce have they fished aboard these airy kings
When, helpless on such unaccustomed floors,
They piteously droop their vast white wings
And trail them at their sides like drifting oars.

How comical, how ugly, and how meek
Appears this soarer of celestial snows:
One with his pipe teases the golden beak,
One, limping, mocks the cripple as he goes.

Like him the shining poet sunward steers,
Whose rushing plumes the hurricanes inflate,
But stranded on the earth to rabble jeers
The great wings of the giant baulk his gait.

41

THE GUM TREES

HALF-HID by leaves, in lofty shoots,
The long lit files of stems arise,
An orchestra of silver flutes
That sing with movement to the eyes:

A movement born of rustling sound,
A rapid stillness, anchored flight,
That far along the level ground
Carries the distance out of sight.

Each interval between their feet
A dryad's stride, as they recede
In immobility more fleet
Than in the whizzing wind of speed,

Far on the sky, with crests aflame,
The tapering avenues unite,
And to a single target aim
The keen velocities of sight;

They snare the eye with clues of speed,
And with the wandering gaze elope:
The sight must follow where they lead,
As running water does the slope;

The impetus their beauty breeds
Is like a silver current hurled
Majestic through the noiseless reeds
Of some less transitory world;

Out of the bounds at which we stick
To what dimensions are they freed
By such superb arithmetic
To multiply their strength and speed?

Along the red-lit rim of space
In lofty cadences they rhyme,
Their march is one victorious race
Of immobility with time;

Far down each rapid colonnade
Their paces cut the shadows white,
They step across their pools of shade
With intervals of silver light;

In shuttered ranks across the gale
They flicker to the moon's white fire,
Like sleepers to an airy rail
They rush beneath her golden tyre;

Softly as a breeze that slumbers

43

They glide across the tufted floor,
For their motion is in numbers
And the shadows are their spoor.

They are the footfalls of the light,
Slippered with rustling leaves they run
Across the darkness of the night
To fetch the white blaze of the sun;

But as the gloom around them fades,
The old hallucination flees,
They swiften through the rushing shades
Their endless marathon of trees;

The winds they wrestled with are thrown,
The miles they trekked are spurned and dead,
But there before the blazing throne
They blacken into shapes of dread,

And on and on without control
Still in the same direction tread:
They, too, have dreamed they sought a goal
When merely from themselves they fled!

Their giant skeletons of shade
Are blackly charred upon the eye,

In motley rags of gloom arrayed
They wear the scorn of earth and sky.

The dusty winds begin to sweep,
The distance stretched before them lies,
Antaeus-like from caves of sleep
Their old antagonists arise.

OVÈRTIME

AMONGST the ponderous tomes of learning,
  Dull texts of medicine and law,
With idle thumb the pages turning
In sudden carnival, I saw,
Revelling forth into the day
In scarlet liveries, nine or ten
Survivors of their own decay—
The flayed anatomies of men:
And marked how well the scalpel's care
Was aided by the painter's tones
To liven with a jaunty air
Their crazy trellises of bones.
In regimental stripes and bands
Each emphasised the cause he serves—
Here was a grenadier of glands
And there a gay hussar of nerves:
And one his skin peeled off as though
A workman's coat with surly shrug
The flexion of the thews to show,
Treading a shovel, grimly dug.
Dour sexton, working overtime,
With gristly toes he hooked his spade
To trench the very marl and slime
In which he should have long been laid.

46

The lucky many of the dead—
Their suit of darkness fits them tight,
Buttoned with stars from foot to head
They wear the uniform of Night;
But some for extra shift are due
Who, slaves for any fool to blame,
With a flayed sole the ages through
Must push the shovel of their fame.